Earth's Precious Resources

Air
A resource our world depends on

Ian Graham

www.heinemann.co.uk/library

Visit our website to find out more information about **Heinemann Library** books.

To order:

☎ Phone 44 (0) 1865 888066

▤ Send a fax to 44 (0) 1865 314091

▢ Visit the Heinemann Bookshop at www.heinemann.co.uk/library to browse our catalogue and order online.

First published in Great Britain by Heinemann Library, Halley Court, Jordan Hill, Oxford OX2 8EJ, part of Harcourt Education.
Heinemann is a registered trademark of Harcourt Education Ltd.

Editorial: Andrew Farrow and Dan Nunn
Design: David Poole and Paul Myerscough
Picture Research: Melissa Allison and Andrea Sadler
Production: Duncan Gilbert

Originated by Ambassador Litho Ltd
Printed in China by WKT Company Limited

ISBN 0 431 11556 7
08 07 06 05 04
10 9 8 7 6 5 4 3 2 1

British Library Cataloguing in Publication Data
Graham, Ian
  Air: a resource our world depends on. –
  (Earth's precious resources)
  1. Air – Juvenile literature
  I. Title
  551.5'1
A full catalogue record for this book is available from the British Library.

Acknowledgements
The publishers would like to thank the following for permission to reproduce photographs: BBC Natural History Unit p. **15 top**; Corbis pp. 6 (Tim Kiusalaas), **10** (Gavin Rowell), **12** (Jim Sugar), **17** (Jim Sugar), **19 top**, **19 bottom** (Charles O'Rear), **20**, **21** (Ralph White), **26 bottom**; FLPA pp. 7 (Hans Dieter Brandl), **23** (W. Wisniewski); Getty Images pp. **5 top** (Taxi), **9 bottom** (Tony Hutchings), **18** (Photodisc); Harcourt Education Ltd pp. **5 bottom**, **9 top**; PA Photos pp. **13**, **29**; Photofusion p. **14** (Liz Somerville); Reuters p. **8** (Andres Stapff); Science Photo Library p. **24** (Adam Hart-Davis); Topham Picturepoint pp. **11** (Photri), **16** (ImageWorks), **22** (ImageWorks), **25** (ImageWorks), **27** (ImageWorks), **28**.

Every effort has been made to contact copyright holders of any material reproduced in this book. Any omissions will be rectified in subsequent printings if notice is given to the publishers.

The paper used to print this book comes from sustainable resources.

Contents

Any words appearing in the text in bold, **like this**, are explained in the Glossary.

What is air?

Air is all around you. It is what you breathe. When you feel the wind against your face, that is air blowing on your skin.

Air is a mixture of different **gases**. Most of the air around you is made of a gas called nitrogen. Oxygen makes up another one-fifth of the air. All of the gases in the air are mixed up together.

What are clouds?

Air also contains some water **vapour**, which is water in the form of a gas. If this moisture cools down, it changes into tiny droplets of water. We see them as clouds. When the droplets are very small, they float in the air. Bigger droplets are too heavy to stay up in the sky and they fall as rain. If they are cold enough, the droplets freeze and change into ice. These may fall as snow or hail.

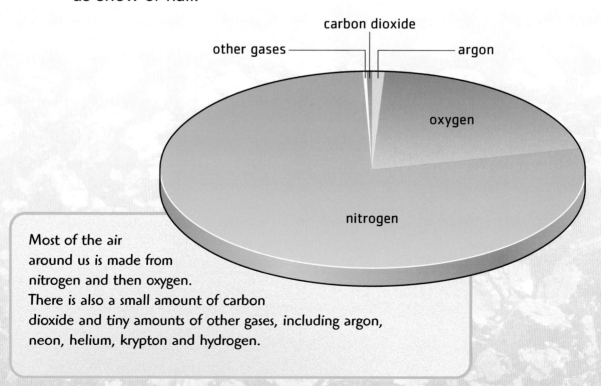

Most of the air around us is made from nitrogen and then oxygen.
There is also a small amount of carbon dioxide and tiny amounts of other gases, including argon, neon, helium, krypton and hydrogen.

What is air pollution?

In some places, air contains extra gases and **smoke**. These are produced by **industry**, vehicles and natural things such as forest fires and **volcanoes**. We call these extra gases and smoke in the air 'pollution'. Most pollution is bad for your health. Air pollution is usually worse in cities, as there is more traffic and industry there.

You can't see air, but you can see its effect on things. Moving air can make a toy windmill spin.

Did you know?

A fluffy summer cloud that is one **kilometre** long, one kilometre wide and one kilometre high contains about 500 tonnes of water!

Clouds are made of water droplets so small that they float in the sky. It takes one **million** droplets to make one raindrop!

Why is air important?

Air is needed by most living things on Earth. Most plants and animals take in air, use the oxygen in it and give out another **gas**, carbon dioxide. Using air like this is called respiration. Animals respire by breathing. Green plants also need air, which they take in through their leaves.

How does air protect us?

The Sun gives out some harmful rays as well as sunlight and heat, which we need. If the harmful rays were to reach us on the ground, they would damage our skin and eyes. But the air around the Earth stops them. It soaks up the most harmful rays before they reach us, but lets the sunlight and heat pass through.

We have to breathe air to stay alive. If this swimmer didn't come up for air, he would probably drown.

How does air affect the temperature on Earth?

Without air, the temperature on the daylight side of the Earth would soar to 100 °C – hot enough to boil water! As soon as the Sun set in the evening, the temperature would quickly drop by 250 degrees to -150 °C. That is 150 degrees colder than ice! Air helps to spread the Sun's heat more evenly around the Earth. It does the same thing in our homes. It helps to spread heat from fires and radiators through the rooms.

Death Valley is the hottest place in the USA. The ground can be as hot as 93.9 °C. It would be even hotter if there was no air blowing across it, carrying some of the heat away.

Did you know?

The Moon has no air to spread the Sun's heat around it. If you could stand on the Moon with one foot in shadow and one in sunlight, one foot would freeze while the other roasted!

Where does the wind come from?

When air warms up, it **expands**, or spreads itself out more thinly. It becomes lighter than the cold air around it and floats upwards. When warm air cools, it sinks back towards the ground. All over the Earth, air is rising in some places and falling in other places. As it rises and falls, the Earth is turning beneath it. All of these movements stir up the air and help to create our weather.

How does wind help plants?

Some plants produce seeds so light that they can be blown about by the wind. This enables them to find new places to grow. Without the wind to carry them away, many seeds would drop next to their parent plants. As all these seeds and plants grew, they would take food, water and light from each other. They would probably not grow very well.

Moving air can be amazingly powerful and destructive. It can blow people over, bring down trees and flatten buildings. Tropical storms called hurricanes and typhoons make winds that blow at more than 120 kilometres (75 miles) per hour – as fast as a family car. Tornadoes are funnels of air that spin at up to 500 kilometres (310 miles) per hour.

Why is air needed for burning?

When something burns, it combines with oxygen in the air and gives out light and heat in the form of a flame. Without oxygen, it would not burn. So one way to put out a fire is to cover it, as this starves it of oxygen. Some fire extinguishers work by smothering a fire with foam, powder or carbon dioxide gas, cutting off its supply of oxygen from the air.

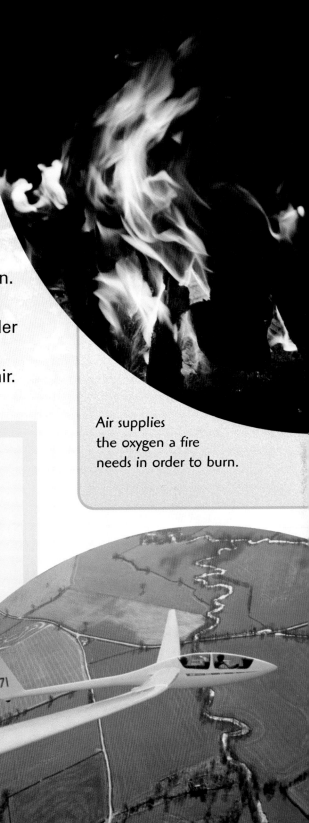

Air supplies the oxygen a fire needs in order to burn.

Did you know?

Rising columns of warm air are called thermals. Glider pilots look for thermals. The rising air carries the glider up with it. A glider can climb thousands of metres high in this way.

Gliders rely on rising air to gain height.

Where is air found?

Air is found all around the Earth. The air around the Earth is known as the **atmosphere**. From space, it looks like a thin blue haze clinging to the Earth.

The lowest part of the atmosphere is where the clouds and weather form and where airliners fly. Higher up, the air gradually thins out. It becomes thinner and thinner until, about 150 **kilometres** (90 miles) above the Earth, there is no air left.

Is air the same everywhere?

The force of gravity that pulls us down to Earth pulls air downwards too. Because of this, air is thicker near the ground and thinner higher up. At the top of a high

Air is so thin at the top of a high mountain that mountaineers often breathe extra oxygen through a face mask.

mountain, there is so little air that it is difficult to get enough oxygen to breathe. Mountaineers who climb the highest mountains usually take extra oxygen with them to help them breathe.

Do all planets have an atmosphere?

Most planets have an atmosphere, but they are not the same as the Earth's. Venus has a very thick atmosphere, made up mainly of carbon dioxide. The giant planet Jupiter has an atmosphere of mainly hydrogen and helium. If you were to go to another planet with a different atmosphere, you would not be able to breathe.

There is no air in space. Astronauts have to take their own atmosphere with them, in their spacecraft or inside their spacesuit.

Did you know?

If all the air around the Earth was collected together and put on a weighing machine, it would weigh 4500 **million** million tonnes.

What can we do to air?

We can do lots of things to air to change the way it looks or how it can be used. We can heat it or cool it, we can squash it up and turn it into a **liquid** or we can clean it.

One of the simplest ways to process air is to heat it or cool it. If air is made very cold and squashed hard, it turns into a liquid. The different substances in liquid air boil at different temperatures. We can use this to separate out the different **gases** in air. If liquid air is allowed to warm up slowly, the nitrogen in it boils first and changes into a gas, which can be collected. Liquid argon boils next and changes into a gas, then oxygen – and in this way all the gases can eventually be separated!

The gases in air can be changed to liquids. This scientist is pouring liquid nitrogen.

Can we clean air?

Air can be cleaned using chemicals. If we keep breathing the same air, we use up the oxygen in it. Very soon, there is not enough oxygen left to breathe. In submarines, the air breathed out by the crew is treated with chemicals to remove the carbon dioxide. Filters also remove any hair and particles of dirt and fluff that are blowing about in the air. Then, with a little fresh oxygen added, the air can be breathed again.

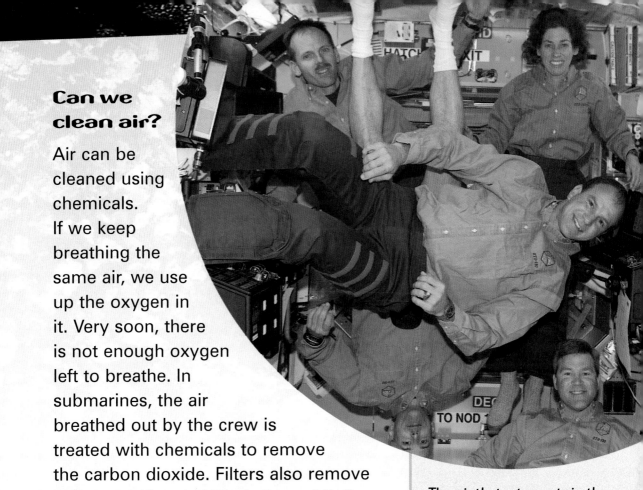

The air that astronauts in the International Space Station breathe is cleaned, mixed with a little new oxygen and then breathed again.

Did you know?

When some gas is changed into a liquid, the liquid takes up far less space than the gas. If 800 **litres** of ordinary air is changed into liquid air, it shrinks so much that it takes up only 1 litre of space.

What is air used for?

Air is used for heating, cooling, drying and filling things up. Bouncy castles, footballs and car tyres get their springiness from the air inside them. The air is squashed inside them so tightly that it pushes outwards in all directions. This pushing is also called pressure.

If air is forced through a pipe by a pump, it can do work. Some tools, including road drills, work by pumped air. An air-powered drill is also called a pneumatic drill.

Air is lighter than water, so things filled with air float. Inflatable boats are made from a rubber tube filled with air.

How does air cool things down?

When cool air blows over something hot, the air soaks up the heat and carries it away. Computers use air to keep cool. A fan sucks in cool air and blows it over the hot parts inside.

Air-filled tyres make a bicycle more comfortable to ride. The springiness of the air soaks up some of the bumps on the ground.

Did you know?

Birds keep warm by fluffing out their feathers to trap air next to their skin.

How does air keep us warm?

Heat always tries to flow from hot to cold, like water flowing downhill. The heat inside a hot house tries to flow to the cold outside. One way to stop this is to have double-glazed windows. This means the windows have two panes of glass instead of one, with a gap between them. The air in the gap acts like a blanket, keeping heat inside the house.

A bear's fur traps a layer of warm air next to its skin, helping to keep out the cold.

How is hot air useful?

Hot air warms things up and dries wet things. When the air in a room is warmed by a heater, it moves around, spreading the warmth to everything it touches. When you have wet hair you can blow it dry with a hair dryer. The hot air from the dryer heats the water on your hair. Then the water changes into a **vapour** and blows away.

gap filled with air or argon gas

glass outside

glass inside

The air-gap in double-glazed windows helps to stop heat leaking out. Sometimes the gap is filled with argon **gas** instead of air, because it is even better at stopping heat leaking out.

How do engines use air?

Most cars, ships and trains move because of what they do to air. They burn fuel to heat up the air inside an engine. Heating air makes it **expand**. It spreads out and takes up more space. When it does this, it pushes with enough force to move parts of the engine. These moving parts are linked to the vehicle's wheels or propellers and make them turn.

What makes a jet engine's jet go?

Jet engines use the power of hot air too, but they work differently from car engines. A big fan at the front of the engine spins and sucks air inside. Some of the air is pushed and squeezed into the middle of the engine, where fuel is burned. The air heats up, expands and rushes out of the back of the engine as a fast, fiery jet. Instead of turning wheels or propellers, it is this jet of air that pushes a jet-plane forwards.

An airliner weighing hundreds of tonnes can be pushed through the sky by the force of hot air!

CASE STUDY:
Altamont Pass wind farm, California, USA

Wind has energy that can be used to do work. A breeze can turn a toy windmill. A stronger wind can turn a bigger windmill. The windmill's spinning blades drive a generator, which produces electricity.

What is a wind farm?

Machines that make electricity from the wind are called wind turbines. A small wind turbine can make electricity for just one house. A large group of much bigger wind turbines can make enough electricity for a whole town. Groups of wind turbines are called wind farms. The world's biggest wind farm is at Altamont Pass, near San Francisco in California, USA. It has more than 7000 wind turbines.

There are more wind turbines at Altamont Pass in the USA than at any other wind farm.

What are the gases in air used for?

Oxygen is one of the most useful **gases** in air. If oxygen is mixed with acetylene (another gas) it burns with a flame that is hot enough to melt metal. When two pieces of metal are held together and melted where they touch, they flow into each other. As they cool down and set hard, the two pieces are joined very strongly. Joining parts in this way is called welding.

Hydrogen is another very useful gas in air. It can be burned in an engine or used to make chemicals. Most of the hydrogen used in **industry** is extracted from natural gas or water.

Nitrogen is used to make some of the chemicals needed by industry. A lot of chemicals contain nitrogen. One of them is ammonia. Ammonia is used to make plant food, some household cleaners and some plastics.

Did you know?

Helium extracted from air is lighter than air, so balloons filled with helium float upwards.

Why is carbon dioxide special?

When most substances are heated, they change from a solid into a **liquid** and then into a gas. Carbon dioxide is different. Solid carbon dioxide changes into a gas without becoming a liquid first. Solid carbon dioxide looks like ice but contains no water, so it is also called dry ice. It is used to keep things cold.

Why do some gases glow?

Neon extracted from air is used in signs that light up shops. When electricity flows through a glass tube filled with neon, the neon gas glows red. Neon tubes are made in different shapes to spell names or make pictures. Other gases are used to make different colours.

The bubbles of gas that appear in a fizzy drink are made from carbon dioxide.

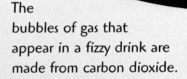

Cities would be much duller places after dark without neon signs.

How is air transported?

Air, or any of the **gases** it contains, can be pumped through pipes or hoses to move it from one place to another. It can also be stored or transported by squashing it tightly into **tanks**. A tank with lots of air, or any other gas, squashed inside it is said to be pressurized.

How do divers breathe underwater?

Most divers breathe air from tanks on their back. Some divers do not wear air tanks. Instead, they breathe air pumped down from the surface through a hose. These divers can move around more easily without big, heavy tanks on their back. They can also stay underwater for longer. Divers with air tanks on their back can stay underwater only for as long as the air in their tanks lasts.

SCUBA divers breathe air from tanks on their back. SCUBA means Self-Contained Underwater Breathing Apparatus.

CASE STUDY: Alvin

Alvin is a type of small submarine called a **submersible**. In 1986, it dived nearly 3960 metres (13,000 feet) into the Atlantic Ocean to explore the wreck of the passenger ship *Titanic*, which sank in 1912. Alvin was one of very few submersibles in the world that could dive so deep without being crushed by the water around it. Alvin's crews use up the air inside it very quickly, so extra oxygen is carried in **tanks** for them to breathe.

How long does Alvin's air last?

Alvin has four oxygen tanks. Less than one tank is used during a normal dive, lasting a few hours. The four tanks contain enough oxygen for its usual crew of three people to breathe for three days.

Alvin supplies its crew with oxygen to breathe while it is underwater.

Will air ever run out?

Air will not run out, because it is not used up. It is constantly **recycled** by plants and animals. Although air cannot run out, it can change. The amounts of the different **gases** in air can change. Air can also be changed by **pollution**. If air becomes very badly polluted all over the world, we could run out of enough clean air to breathe.

Has the air always been the same?

Air was different in the past. Before there were any plants on Earth, there was no oxygen in the **atmosphere**. It was locked up inside other chemicals. Plants changed the atmosphere by unlocking the oxygen and letting it go into the air. Trees and other plants are still doing this today.

The erupting Popocatepetl **volcano** in Mexico (shown here in 2000) poured out enormous amounts of gas, but the atmosphere is so big that the volcano's gases were like a few drops of ink poured into a bath of water.

How can the air be changed?

When plants die and rot, or when they burn, they give off carbon dioxide. **Millions** upon millions of trees and other plants would have to die or catch fire at the same time to change the air all around the world. Only an enormous disaster affecting the whole planet could do this – for example, a giant asteroid (a rock from space) crashing into the Earth.

How are people changing the air today?

Some of the things that people do can affect the atmosphere. Vehicles and **industry** pollute the air with **smoke** and gases. Fires started to clear land and to burn old crops send smoke and carbon dioxide into the air. When fires were started in Indonesia in 1997, they spread out of control. Smoke covered Indonesia and several other countries. It even reached Australia!

Forests recycle gases in the Earth's atmosphere. During the day, plant leaves absorb carbon dioxide and give out oxygen. At night, they do the opposite.

Why should we look after the air?

It is important to look after air, because we cannot do without it. Some **industries** produce **smoke** and **gases** that change the natural balance of the gases in air. Some of them are harmless, but others can make it harder to breathe. Some of them are poisonous or cause illnesses such as **cancer**. It is important to reduce air **pollution** as much as possible and to keep air clean.

Why is air pollution such a serious problem?

Air pollution does not stay in one place. Wind can blow it a long way, so that it affects other places. Smoke and **fumes**

Buildings in big cities have to be cleaned, because pollution from traffic, factories and fires settles on them and makes them dirty.

from factories in one country can blow over another country. The gases may mix with moisture in the air and form **acids**. When these acids fall as rain, they can kill forests and damage buildings by eating away the stone they are made from.

Is air pollution getting better or worse?

There are more industries and traffic today than ever before. However, many cities have cleaner air now than they had 100 years ago. At that time, many people heated their homes by burning coal, which produced thick black smoke. Sometimes, this smoke mixed with **fog** to make a choking mixture called smog. Today, air is cleaner because few people burn coal, industries are not allowed to pour smoke and fumes into the air, and vehicles have cleaner engines.

Did you know?

Mexico City is one of the world's most polluted cities. This is because it is surrounded by mountains that stop the wind from blowing the pollution away.

CASE STUDY: Global warming

Some **gases** are called **greenhouse gases**, because they soak up heat from the Sun, like a greenhouse. Greenhouse gases include carbon dioxide and methane. If the **atmosphere** contains more of these gases, it traps more heat and warms up. This is called **global warming**, because it affects the whole world.

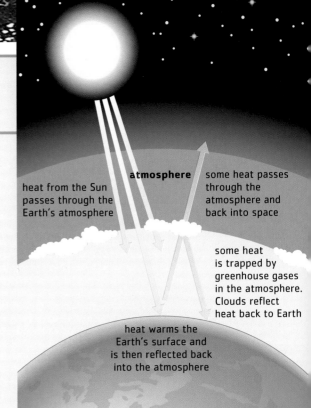

heat from the Sun passes through the Earth's atmosphere

atmosphere

some heat passes through the atmosphere and back into space

some heat is trapped by greenhouse gases in the atmosphere. Clouds reflect heat back to Earth

heat warms the Earth's surface and is then reflected back into the atmosphere

Earth

Why is global warming bad for us?

A warmer atmosphere changes our weather. Most scientists believe this is happening now. The gases produced by **industry** and traffic may be warming the atmosphere and making storms, floods and **droughts** worse.

Greenhouse gases trap heat from the Sun and stop it escaping into space.

Did you know?

Nearly half of the greenhouse gases produced by New Zealand come from its 50 **million** sheep 'burping'!

How can we look after the air?

There are several ways of looking after our precious air. We can look for ways of reducing air **pollution**. We can also protect the world's great forests, such as the Amazon rainforest in South America, so that they carry on **recycling** the air and producing fresh oxygen.

How can we reduce air pollution?

One way of reducing air pollution is to change to cleaner ways of making electricity. Making electricity from the wind produces less pollution than burning coal or oil. Another way to reduce pollution is to use less electricity. We could make our homes less draughty so that we need less energy to heat them. We could also use lights, washing machines, fridges and freezers that are designed to use less electricity.

So many trees are cut down every year that it is important to plant more to replace them.

How can we make traffic less polluting?

We could make fewer journeys by car, perhaps by using public transport whenever possible. Car-makers could design engines that produce less pollution. We could use engines that burn cleaner fuels, such as hydrogen. When hydrogen burns, it produces nothing more harmful than water.

How does industry reduce air pollution?

In many countries, **industries** are not allowed to send all the **smoke** and waste **gases** they produce up chimneys into the air. The chimneys are fitted with filters that trap most of the sooty particles in the smoke. The smoke may also be treated with chemicals to remove harmful gases.

Small boxes fixed to poles in many towns and cities today measure the air to check how clean it is.

CASE STUDY:
The Kyoto Treaty

Governments meet regularly to discuss how the land, sea and air are affected by what people do. They decide what should be done to protect the Earth. In 1997, governments met in Kyoto, Japan, to decide what to do about **global warming**. They decided to cut the amount of **greenhouse gases** that countries produce. Their agreement is called the Kyoto **Treaty**.

Is the Kyoto Treaty working?

In 2001, some countries were unhappy with the Kyoto Treaty. It forced their power stations and industries to burn less coal and oil. Poorer countries trying to provide more power, water and transport need more electricity and vehicles, but these would produce more greenhouse gases, not less. It is harder for these countries to stick to the treaty. After more discussion, 180 countries agreed that some countries should reduce their greenhouse gases more than others.

Here, Canadian Prime Minister Jean Chrétien is pictured signing the Kyoto Treaty.

Glossary

acids substances that contain hydrogen and dissolve in water. Weak acids have a sour taste. Strong acids eat into other materials. Oranges and lemons contain citric acid. Vinegar contains ascetic acid. Your stomach contains acid to help digest food.

atmosphere the mixture of gases that surround a planet or a moon

cancer medical condition that involves cells multiplying (growing in numbers) out of control

drought long period of time when there is no rain, leaving the ground too dry to grow plants. A drought can last for a few weeks, months or even years.

expand get bigger. When a gas expands, it fills a bigger space.

fog white cloud that floats near the ground. It is made of countless tiny water droplets floating about in air.

fumes harmful gas or smoke

gas substance that expands to fill its container. Nitrogen and oxygen are the main gases in air.

global warming rise in the temperature of the Earth's atmosphere due to the greenhouse effect

greenhouse gas gas that absorbs heat from the Sun and helps to warm the atmosphere. This warming is called the greenhouse effect.

industry businesses involved with extracting or processing materials or making goods

kilometre distance equal to 1000 metres (3280 feet)

liquid substance that flows and takes up the shape of any container it is poured into. Water is a liquid.

litre amount of space that 1 kilogram of water takes up. That's about the size of a large grapefruit or a small pumpkin.

million very big number, equal to one thousand thousands

pollution harmful or poisonous substances in nature, especially those produced by the activities of people

recycle use things again instead of using them only once and then throwing them away

smoke cloud of tiny particles hanging in the air

submersible small submarine. Submersibles cannot travel very far on their own. They have to be carried by a ship to the place where they dive.

tank container for holding liquids or gases

treaty agreement signed between two or more countries

vapour gas that can be changed into a liquid just by squashing it

volcano hole in the Earth's crust where lava (liquid rock) explodes, sprays or pours out

Find out more

Books

Experiment With Air, Bryan Murphy (Two-Can Publishing, 2002)

I Can Help Clean Our Air, V. Smith (Franklin Watts, 2001)

Up in the Air, Wendy Madgwick (Hodder Wayland, 1998)

Websites

www.epa.gov/airnow/aqikids

This is Koko Chameleon's guide to air, from the US Environmental Protection Agency.

www.epa.gov/globalwarming/kids

This US Environmental Protection Agency site tells you all about global warming.

www.hcdoes.org/airquality/kids/home.htm

This is a guide to air pollution and conservation (ways of protecting the environment).

Index

Titles in the *Earth's Precious Resources* series include:

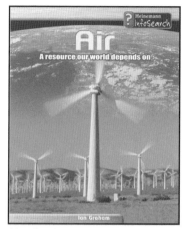

Hardback   0 431 11556 7

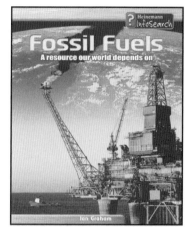

Hardback   0 431 11550 8

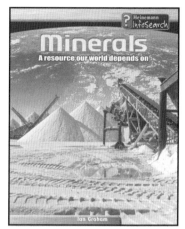

Hardback   0 431 11552 4

Hardback   0 431 11551 6

Hardback   0 431 11553 2

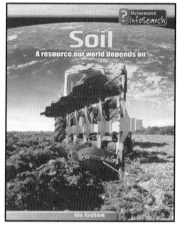

Hardback   0 431 11554 0

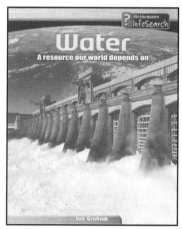

Hardback   0 431 11555 9

Find out about the other titles in this series on our website www.heinemann.co.uk/library